For my family and yours; we're all in this together —S. M.

For my family, my very own little world —D. L.

For the aardvarks —E.

Henry Holt and Company, *Publishers since 1866*
Henry Holt® is a registered trademark of Macmillan Publishing Group, LLC
120 Broadway, New York, NY 10271 • mackids.com

Library of Congress Control Number: 2021917046

Our books may be purchased in bulk for promotional, educational, or business use.
Please contact your local bookseller or the Macmillan Corporate and Premium Sales Department at
(800) 221-7945 ext. 5442 or by email at MacmillanSpecialMarkets@macmillan.com.

First edition, 2022
Book design by Cindy De la Cruz
The illustrations for this book were created using mixed media and digital art tools.
Printed and bound in Mexico by Procesos y Acabados en Artes Gráficas S.A. de C.V.

ISBN 978-1-250-78249-6 (hardcover)

5 7 9 10 8 6 4

OUR UNIVERSE

OUR PLANET!

THERE'S NO PLACE LIKE EARTH

BY Earth (WITH STACY McANULTY)

ILLUSTRATED BY Earth (AND DAVID LITCHFIELD)

Henry Holt and Company ✳ New York

Hi! I'm **EaRth**.
Also known as Planet Awesome.
Also known as *your* awesome home.

Actually, I'm home to *all* the plants in the solar system and *all* the animals, including *all* the humans. That's nearly eight billion people.

Where else would you want to live?
Where else could you live?

On one of my
seven siblings?

Saturn

Mars?
He's too cold.
(All his water is frozen.)

Neptune

Uranus

Reasons I'm a perfect home planet
(besides all my oxygen, water, and ice cream):

Distance from the Sun.
An ideal 93 million miles in a zone that's
not too hot and not too cold.

My massive Ocean.
Absorbs extra heat,
helps make oxygen,
and is very pretty.

And my atmosphere.
A blanket of gases
that wraps me—
and you—in a
gentle hug.
Hugs are nice.

Without my atmosphere, my **CLIMATE** would be wacky and not good for flora (that's plants) and fauna (that's animals, like you!).

30 Years Ago

Present

30 Years From Now

I'm Earth with your climate forecast.

CLIMATE: Seasonal weather over a long time, like thirty years, and in a big region

Climate is not the same as weather.

Weather: Now or very soon and in a specific place

When climate does change, it should be slooooooooooooooooow. Like 700 million years ago, when I was a giant snowball for a loooooong time.

Or 55 million years ago, when I was nearly ice-free for a looooooong time. Crocodile-like creatures lived near the North Pole.

But humans have accidentally moved
my climate into the fast lane. I'm
getting warm super quick.

Uh-oh.

It's because so many human things need energy.
Energy to make them.
Energy to move them.
Energy to use them.

Sometimes energy leads
to dirty water, dirty land,
and dirty air.

My atmosphere is getting messy, and this new blanket is very uncomfortable. It's making me sweaty!

Icebergs are melting.

Oceans are rising.

Some land is flooding.

Other land is too
dry and hot.

Yikes!
Not good.

Weather is getting wild.

Heat waves are dangerous.

Big-time troubles.

And when I'm in trouble,
Earthlings are in trouble, too.

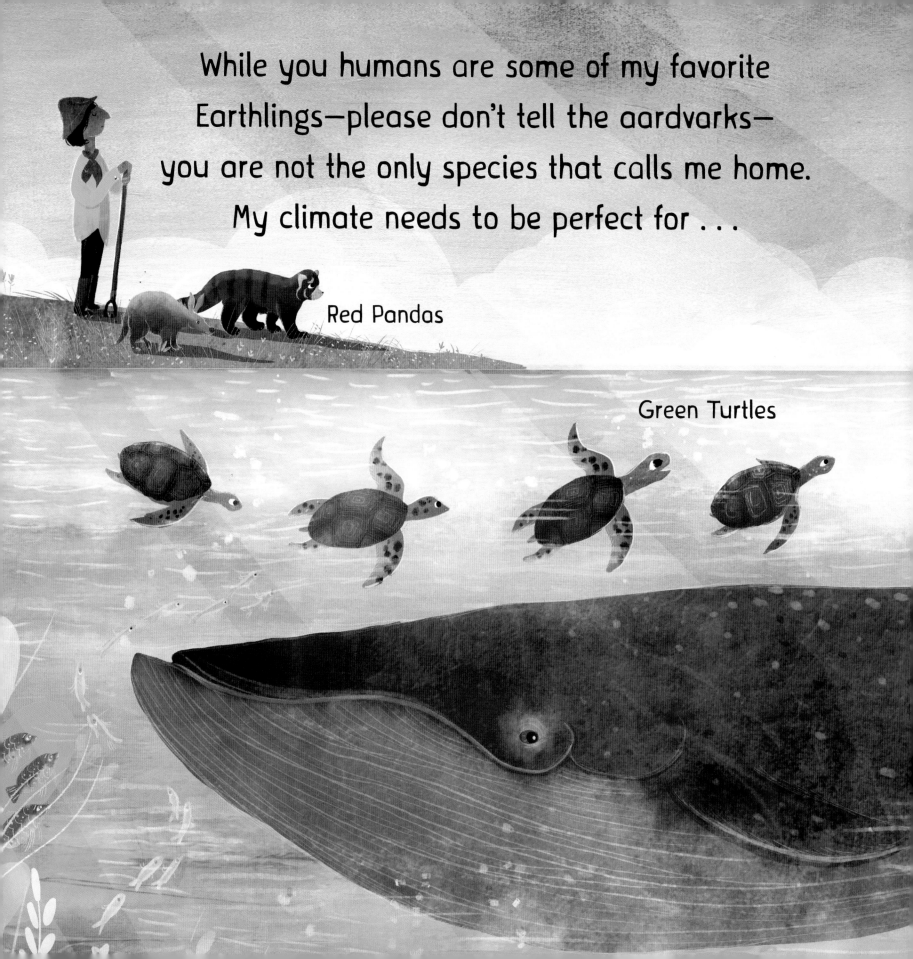

While you humans are some of my favorite
Earthlings—please don't tell the aardvarks—
you are not the only species that calls me home.
My climate needs to be perfect for . . .

Red Pandas

Green Turtles

Black Rhinos

Blue Whales

Great White Sharks

Keep Earth colorful!

Good news!
It's not too late!

We can stop passing the gas.

Let me introduce some cleaner energies.

Wind power—
that's from,
you guessed it, wind.

Hydropower—
that's from moving water.

Human power—
that's from your own two feet.

Solar power—
that's from Sun.

Humans can share stuff,

make and buy less new stuff,

reuse the old stuff,

and recycle the
worn-out stuff.

And let's make more
room for flora.
Trees are good for cleaning
the air, cooling off,
and climbing high.

There's no other planet like me in the solar system.
And I need your help to stay awesome.

Earthlings need me,
and I need Earthlings.

We still Love you, Earth!

I hope so!

Dear Fellow Earthlings,

Don't you love our planet with all her fabulous gifts? From water to oxygen, from food to shelter, from books to video games, she supplies it all (or the resources needed to *make* it all). Everything we want or need comes from Earth. If we all moved to Mars or Pluto, we'd have to bring everything with us, including breathable air. That's why we have to take care of this planet and keep her atmosphere and water clean and not use up all the resources. It's not going to be easy. But working together, we can be the best humans Earth has ever seen.

Sincerely,

Stacy McAnulty
Author and proud inhabitant of Earth

P.S. Scientists are learning more and more about our awesome planet all the time. That means some of what we know now may change, and that's okay. Our species is getting smarter.

Earth by the Numbers

7,800,000,000 — Earth's human population was approximately 7.8 billion in 2020.

23,000,000,000 — Earth's chicken population was 23 billion in 2018, and most chickens are raised for food.

115°F — Death Valley is the hottest spot on the planet and has an average high of 115°F.

−128.6°F — The lowest recorded temperature in Antarctica was a chilly −128.6°F.

57°F — Earth's average temperature was a lovely 57°F through the twentieth century.

2.7°F — If the planet's temperature rises more than 2.7°F, Earth will not be a healthy home for humans and other animals.

93,000,000 — Sun is a perfect (but slightly varying) 93 million miles from Earth.

An Awesome Atmosphere

A Giant Blanket: Earth is surrounded by a layer of gases called an atmosphere. It lets in heat and light from Sun and keeps some of the heat from escaping back into space.

Key Ingredients: Our atmosphere is mostly nitrogen and oxygen, though we can also find greenhouse gases (GHGs) like carbon dioxide (CO_2), methane (CH_4), nitrous oxide (N_2O), and others. These GHGs are okay at certain levels, but when the amounts increase even a little bit, it has quite an impact on Earth.

Carbon Dioxide Creators: When we burn fuel like oil, coal, and gas, we produce CO_2 waste (and other GHGs). These fuels power our factories, homes, schools, vehicles, farms, and more.

Ups and Downs: When carbon dioxide increases in our atmosphere, the average temperature on Earth goes up. When carbon dioxide goes down, so does the temperature.

Cow Gas: Cattle belch and toot methane gas. (Cow burps are more of a problem than cow farts.) Methane is not good for the atmosphere and can make our planet too warm.

Just Right: Earth's average temperature is just right for humans. But to keep it from getting too warm, we need to watch how much CO_2 and other GHGs we put into the air.

What Earthlings Can Do

Use Less Energy at Home: It takes a lot of electricity to heat and cool and power our homes. We can cut back by turning off lights and gadgets when we're not using them and keeping our space a little warmer in the summer (less air-conditioning) and a little cooler in the winter (less heat).

Transportation Choices: Cars, planes, buses, trains, and big boats can burn lots of fuel. We can use less by sharing rides and not keeping the car running while we wait.

Buy Less New Stuff: Most of what we own comes from factories, from our toys to our clothes to our electronics. Factories need energy and often use lots of fuel. We can choose to have fewer items, or we can buy secondhand stuff.

Give Away (or Sell) Old Stuff: When we outgrow something or just don't need it anymore, it is better to donate it (or sell it) than put it in the landfill.

Eat More Veggies and Fruits: Meat and other animal products like eggs, cheese, and milk have a big impact on the environment compared to vegetables, grains, and non-animal products. If we eat less meats, we will help Earth and be healthier.

Learn More: There are serious problems threatening Earth, and the solutions require significant changes from Earthlings. Let's continue learning more about our world and our climate, and then we can keep our planet healthy and have a beautiful home for millions of years to come.

Sources

Bada, Ferdinand. "The Coldest Places on Earth." WorldAtlas.com. December 06, 2018. https://www.worldatlas.com/articles/what-is-the-coldest-place-on-earth.html.

Fountain, Henry. "Climate Change Is Accelerating, Bringing World 'Dangerously Close' to Irreversible Change." *New York Times*. December 04, 2019. https://www.nytimes.com/2019/12/04/climate/climate-change-acceleration.html.

Kiprop, Victor. "Where Is the Hottest Place on Earth?" WorldAtlas.com. December 13, 2018. https://www.worldatlas.com/articles/where-is-the-hottest-place-on-earth.html.

Lindsey, Rebecca, and LuAnn Dahlman. "Climate Change: Global Temperature." NOAA Climate.gov. August 14, 2020. https://www.climate.gov/news-features/understanding-climate/climate-change-global-temperature.

"Overview: Weather, Global Warming, and Climate Change." NASA Global Climate Change: Vital Signs of the Planet. August 28, 2019. https://climate.nasa.gov/resources/global-warming-vs-climate-change/.

Scott, Michon, and Rebecca Lindsey. "What's the Hottest Earth's Ever Been?" NOAA Climate.gov. June 18, 2020. https://www.climate.gov/news-features/climate-qa/whats-hottest-earths-ever-been.

Sneed, Annie. "A New Idea on How Earth Became a Giant Snowball." *Scientific American*. May 08, 2017. https://www.scientificamerican.com/article/a-new-idea-on-how-earth-became-a-giant-snowball/.